ADDICT

SIGNS, STORIES & SAYINGS

A Life Told Through Signs, Struggles, and Survival

A. Mustafa Tut Brown Jr.

Dedication

To my parents, Vincent Brown and Idaline Benjamin-Brown, whose love, decisions, and sacrifices made my life possible.

My father lived like a worker bee, rising before dawn six days a week to till the soil and resting only when the sun fell. My mother worked her hands to the bone, her life a rhythm of effort and endurance.

Though they are both gone, their spirit remains my foundation.

To my sister Louise, who became my second mother; to Danny and Noel, my brothers in blood and spirit; to friends Oliver, Leon, Dami, Colin, and Shepherd; and to my children Noni, Abenen, Mustafa Q, Akasua, Kai, and Malik, this book is for you. You are the living signs of my life's meaning. Thanks

Acknowledgment

This book exists because of every experience, every failure, every risk, and every moment of grace that shaped my life.

First and always, I thank God for the strength to endure, the insight to grow, and the purpose to serve. I am deeply grateful for my children—my six greatest teachers—whose lives give meaning to my work and whose futures inspire every day I work and every word I write. You are my reason, my mirror, and my motivation to still be here and still trying to make something more of myself.

I acknowledge every season since 1986 that tested me through business, the hustles, setbacks, and all the hard-earned lessons— in the lease and finance industry, the trucking, cargo transport businesses, not to mention the demolition, construction, renovation and consulting attempts, and so much more. Each chapter refined me. I would not change a single step. I own it all.

To those who supported me when I had nothing—especially during my darkest season in especially in 2006, when I was bankrupt, alone, lost home and family and living in my car—your belief carried me when my own strength was fading. Those moments became the turning point that revealed my true calling: to help people rise, solve real problems, and become their best selves.

I honor every client, every conversation, and every life that trusted me with their truth. You taught me that coaching is not a profession—it is a responsibility.

To the giants of film, art, and storytelling who inspired me to see life as a narrative of struggle, redemption, and transformation— thank you for lighting the path.

Finally, I thank every reader who have and will opened this book searching for clarity, meaning, and direction. I hope that *Addict, Signs, Stories & Sayings* helps you awaken the hero within yourself, to challenge all comfortable and uncomfortable limitations, and step toward more than you once believed possible.

With gratitude,

A. Mustafa Tut Brown Jr.

Contents

Preface

This book took me twenty years to write, maybe more.

Between births, deaths, marriages, businesses, and breakdowns, life kept interrupting me. Every chapter was lived before it was written.

I lost family, friends, and faith along the way, but I also found myself.

The title changed as I did: Signs, then Stories, Signs & Sayings, then Addicted, Signs, and Sayings. Maybe that's life, a constant rewrite.

I've come to believe the signs are always there, birth and death, sunshine and rain, beginnings and endings. The stories never stop. We just keep living, writing and reading new chapters.

Objective

My goal isn't to preach. I'm just telling my truth through the lens f a man who has fallen, hard and deep, climbed back up, and learned to see meaning in the chaos. Like Jonah, I ran from my calling. like everyone, I was swallowed by my own storms. But divine grace gave me another chance. This book is part of my second chance to speak, to share, to serve, to get it right

"I don't throw stones because I've been living in a glass house, and I've got skeletons in all my closets."

That line sums me up better than any biography could. A long time ago, while in university, I hosted a radio talk show. I learned a lot behind that microphone about how words can travel far, how thoughts can shape people, and how truth can make you both friends and enemies. One day, I said something that changed everything. I told listeners to:

"Quit your job and start your own business now."

That single statement got me kicked off the air. The dean and station manager called it *irresponsible*. Looking back, maybe it was or maybe I was right. Since that day i have met people who heard me on air and said they appreciated me saying those words, because that single radio moment changed their life.

That moment taught me a lasting truth: **words carry weight**. They can build or destroy, inspire or offend. So, when I first thought about writing this book, I wanted to just speak freely, say whatever came to mind. But then I remembered that microphone, that red light and that quiet voice reminding me: *think before you speak.*

So I did. I thought deeply. And I wrote carefully.

A Life Lived in Motion and in Falling

The story you're about to read is not a theory. It's life, lived raw and unfiltered.

I've fallen on my face hard,. I've crashed through the floor, broken bones and broken businesses, and yes broken hearts. I've lost marriages, relationships, and money. I've started over more times than I can count.

In many ways, my life mirrors Jonah's, the man who ran from his divine calling, only to end up in the belly of a whale. I, too, ran from purpose. I hid behind work, money, movement, and noise. I flew high and far, chasing success like it was oxygen. Then one day, I crashed, grounded, breathless, and unable to walk.

That's when I learned the hardest truth of all: *flying isn't living*. You have to walk your path one step at a time.

The Fall and
the Awakening

When the ground gave way beneath me, I fell into darkness, a pit filled with noise, judgment, and the echoes of my critics. I heard voices laugh:

"Good for you. It's karma."

"You're done. Give up now."

But I didn't. Because deep down, I still had one thing left, a belief that I could try again. That even after failure, there's a chapter waiting to be written.

In that pit, I remembered something: I've always had *the gift of the gab*, a way with people and words, and an ability to connect, to motivate, to help. Yet for years, I ran from that gift. I chased money, business, and survival instead. I built companies in logistics, construction, finance, and restaurants. Each venture was a classroom and that each failure was a lesson.

What kept me going was a single question I once heard from a female speaker, a spark that changed my life:

"Have you ever thought about starting your own business?"

That question lit the fuse. It sent me tumbling through decades of hustle and reinvention. I didn't know it then, but I wasn't chasing success; I was chasing *meaning*. I was addicted to the struggle, not the prize.

The Real

Reason for

This Book

Today, after all the crashes and comebacks, I see the signs clearly. Every failure, every loss, every sleepless night, they were all messages pointing me back to my true purpose.

This book is that purpose reborn.

It's not a lecture or a sermon. It's a mirror. I'm sharing these stories so that someone out there, maybe you, will see yourself in these reflections and realize that failure isn't final.

My hope is simple: That even one word, one story, or one sign in these pages will inspire someone to wake up to see their own gifts, embrace their truth, and become everything the universe (or God) destined them to be.

Because if I've learned anything, it's this:

We all get second chances. The question is, what will we do with them?

Book I

Mustafa Tut Brown

Chapter 1

The Rocky

Road

Some people have trouble waking up at five am in the morning.

Not me.

Back home, I remember waking up at five a.m. every day to fetch firewood, then walking miles to the water pipe to get water for cooking. I carried the buckets of water and the firewood on my tiny head, talk about balancing skills.

After that came the goats. I had to take them out to the green fields, bring them back, sweep the yard, and cut grass for the pigs. All of that had to be done **before** I could wash up, eat breakfast, and make it to school, hopefully before the headmaster caught me at the gate with her whip in hand.

My Father, the Quiet Man

There's that old song that goes,

"Papa was a rolling stone; wherever he laid his hat was his home."

Ok, yeah, but that wasn't my father.

My father built his home with his own hands, and I was born in it. It's still standing today.

I don't have many real memories of him. He died when I was around seven or eight years old. He wasn't a talker; more of a quiet man. I don't even remember the sound of his voice, only his laughter on rare occasions.

He was what people called a **subsistence farmer** planting sugar cane, yams, and coffee. I remember him coming home from the fields exhausted, smelling like a musty gym bag or a pair of sweaty shoes. He'd sit on a tree stump in the yard, have something hot to drink, let out a long burp, then clean up and eat dinner.

Sometimes, before bedtime, he'd call us together and grill us about school stuff. We had to recite the ABCs, count to a thousand, and run through the multiplication tables. *Good times, right?*

Not exactly.

The Wedding Day

I vividly remember the day my father married my mother. That was the first *real* memory I have of her.

My younger brother and I fought that day, I can't even remember why. But I know that I lost the fight, and ended up with a cut above my eye, it bled like crazy i thought i lost my eye, I see the scar every time I look in the mirror. The blood ruined my mother's wedding dress which made my father so furious; he took the belt to us.

That's when I fell in love for the first time.

My mother, a little woman barely four feet one inches tall, she stepped between us and my father's belt. She took the blows meant for us. She cleaned my wound, calmed the storm, and somehow, the wedding continued.

From that day forward, she was my first hero.

The Belt and the Bible

My father believed in discipline, the kind you felt.

Sometimes, he'd wait until we were in bed, half-asleep, and then appear in the doorway, belt in hand. He didn't raise his voice; he just did what he thought was right. I still remember the sting.

I remember shining my shoes for Sunday church. I remember the day he died. I saw his body for the last time in that same church.

I wasn't sad. The heavy hand had fallen; he died.

After the Funeral

After he passed, my mother went overseas to work. That left us without a father or a mother. We bounced from one relative's house to another, facing the cruelty of adults who thought they had the right to punish us for every little thing.

Looking back, it all seems so pointless.

Why not just talk to a child?...Offer some kind words and some direction? Instead, we got belts and whips and occasionally, a barrel from our mother filled with clothes and treats, distractions to make up for her absence.

Then came what I thought would be the best day of my life, the day my mother returned to take us to Canada. I was so excited I could barely sleep.

But when she came, she only took the older ones.

That was the first heartbreak I can remember, deep, raw, and unforgettable. My brother and I cried our eyes out, running alongside the car as it left the yard. Even now, as I write these words, I can still feel that ache in my chest.

We waited three long years before she returned to get us. When she finally did, it was bittersweet. We were leaving behind my sister, the only real mother we'd known, to go live with the mother we *wished* we had.

Becoming a Teen

At thirteen years old, I was that skinny kid in grade school who was always joking, chatting, and smiling. Maybe you knew a kid like that, the funny one who never seemed to take life seriously.

But underneath all that laughter was insecurity.

I was small, barely five feet tall, maybe a hundred pounds soaking wet. I wasn't fashionable. I wasn't the kid the girls called "cute" or "handsome." I wasn't picked first for teams or invited to the best parties.

To everyone else, I looked happy-go-lucky. Inside, I was drowning in self-doubt.

Maybe I was just a normal teen. Those were the years when the *real* struggles began.

Losing and Finding Mothers

I loved my grandmother. She was the first real mother I knew. When she passed, I cried for a long time. I felt alone and abandoned.

After my father's death, I stayed with my sister, who became my stand-in mother. Her husband was an ass kicker, too, just like our father was.

But, you know, when I finally moved to live with my real mother in Canada, it wasn't the reunion I had dreamed of. I did not know who she was.

She worked long hours, often late into the night. We rarely talked. The home was tense, a constant battle over cleaning duties, dishes, and who took control of the TV remote.

I was the second youngest, which meant I didn't get much say in anything. I hated it.

School was my escape. Or at least, lunch break was. Gym was my favorite subject; academics, not so much. I was suspended even expelled, once. I remember cussing out the principal. My mother marched to the school and made them take me back.

But it didn't last.

A month before graduation, I got into another fight, this time with my brothers, over dishes or TV, something trivial. My mother stood there watching as we wrestled on the floor.

That was it. I saw the disappointment in her eyes, and I realized she wasn't on my side.

That night, I left home for good.

The First Step Out

I had nowhere to go, just the clothes on my back and a few dollars saved from summer work. I walked through the night until I saw a sign that read:

Bachelor Apartment for Rent.

I waited for the rental office to open and I rented it on the spot.

That was my first real step into the world of obligation, scared, unsure, but I fell that I was finally free.

(Side note: I did go back to night school later to try and finish secondary school.)

Chapter 2

College Was a Daydream (Sort Of)

College was, to me, a daydream sort of. It was not much different from high school. My head was not in it; I had no clear idea what I wanted to study or become. It felt as if I was simply there because I could be, passing the time, drifting along the stream of life.

Many years later, I would return to university, spending three years studying philosophy, followed by a diploma in mental health and addictions. Back then, however, I was still searching, my thoughts were scattered, flying in all directions almost like daydreams.

One thing I did know was that I had a quick mind. I was a problem solver, a word conjurer. I had what people call the gift of the gab I could weave words together like a spider spins its web. That talent helped me immensely in conversation and in persuasion. To this day, my phone rings with people seeking advice or solutions. It seems I've always been the one people called when they're in trouble and needed a fix.

The Experiment That Changed Everything

That college experiment didn't last long.

At the tender age of nineteen, I moved out on my own, and to be honest, getting into business saved my life.

How, you ask? Well, there I was, sitting at home, heartbroken over the love of my life having dumped me, when the phone rang. It was an old friend named Dianne. She invited me to a small business conference in the city. That call changed the trajectory of my life.

I went.

At the conference, a woman speaker took the stage. As she spoke, she suddenly stopped, then pointed directly at me. "You there!" she shouted.

I looked around, startled. "Me?"

"Yes, you!" she said, walking toward me. "Have you ever thought about having your own business?"

With a blank and surprised look, I said, "No."

That moment was like pouring ten spoons of sugar into coffee a sudden jolt of energy and realization.

She smiled, stepped off the stage, handed me her business card, and said, "Call me Monday morning at 10 a.m."

Still in shock, I took the card. I called.

That call became the most important one of my life. I met with her, and the rest, as they say, is history. Till today, I don't think she knows she changed my life and how much I appreciate her for that.

Chapter 3

Discovering

Focus Through

Business

Business gave me something to focus on a place to channel my restless energy and forget my emotional pain. It became my new love interest.

Here name is Nazima, she taught me the basics: "We ship things in containers and crates, by sea, to wherever 'home' is," she said. "Just find people who want to send goods back home and call me with the details, I'll help you make it happen."

It sounded simple enough, exciting even. although I had no clue what I was getting into.

Starting a business, I soon discovered, is the easy part. Staying in business, well that's an entirely different story. It's the most difficult, most humbling, and most character-defining challenge there is. You must be mentally prepared to do whatever it takes to keep the business dream alive. Energy alone is not enough.

Let's rewind for a moment. It was 1986 or '87 when I started my first business. I had no cash in my bank account or my pockets, and I had no business plan just excitement, passion, and credit cards. I maxed them all to fund my start-up.

I had a driver's license, but no car, just a bicycle, so. I rode that bike all over the city till the wheels busted, promoting my new transport and moving business. It was fun, yes but also very gruelling. Looking back now, I can freely admit this, I was very unprepared.

Eventually, the bell went off, I read the writing on the wall, I realized that I wasn't built for all that heavy labourers lifting work, my body was being destroyed. So to help solve that problem, I took on a partner who had a couple of trucks. yes, I thought that would solve my problems. It didn't. The problem doubled, and then add dealing with another personality and the financial splits and, and, and , the stress was overwhelming. I called it a day and closed the business

I turned my attention to a new path, finance, as a financial consultant, where I hoped to use my mind instead of my muscles.

Truth Be Told

I've tried real estate development and renovations didn't work. I'm not a "nail and hammer" guy. I overextended myself and ended up in a spectacular collapse. Then the cafés, nightclubs, fast food ventures in the hospitality sector, same results: total disaster.

I even tried financial and insurance consulting, no luck there either. And then, back again to shipping and transport six trucks this time. You'd think that I did learn, right. but no, it was a total disaster.

High insurance costs, constant breakdowns, rising fuel prices, unreliable drivers, endless stress. My hair turned white and began to fall out. Every day felt like pushing a giant boulder uphill.

I dreaded those 3 a.m. phone calls where the driver says to me,

"The truck crashed." I blow a tire; the gas card is not working

"The load is lost." I am late to deliver.

I tell you, I began to hate the business, the stress became my shadow.

Some days, I wanted to crawl under a blanket and sleep till the year twenty fifty five or just disappear. Other days, I thought about buying a one-way plane ticket and leaving it all behind. But I didn't. My ego wouldn't let me and honestly, plane tickets are expensive to Zimbabwe, plus I had no money for a plane ticket anyway.

Look, everyone has heard the phrase "skeletons in the closet."

Well, I have so many that the closet can't close anymore.

I'm a serial entrepreneur and I've made every mistake you can imagine. For every one success, there have been ten, maybe twenty, setbacks. I prefer to call them "setbacks" rather than "failures."

On Curses and Choices

A friend once told me he thought he was cursed because nothing ever worked out for him. For a moment, I wondered if I was cursed, too. But I quickly dismissed it. A curse couldn't possibly explain why only my life, my business ventures struggled, while everyone else was fine.

No, the problem wasn't a curse. It was me, I just wasn't on the right path. You can't ride smoothly when you're not on the right road.

So, I sucked it up and started again. People say, "Get up and do it again," "shake it off" "forget about" but they never tell you how hard that actually is.

So, I got up risked everything again and again thinking "next time it'll work." That mindset is absolutely necessary for entrepreneurs. You have to believe that next one good push will finally get the boat across the river.

Owning the Dream

I tried blaming others. I played the anger game. But in the end, I couldn't blame anyone but myself.

It was my dream, not theirs; I had to own the fail.

Most people just want a pay check; it's rare to find someone who shares your vision enough to invest their own time or money. So, when things fail, the blame falls entirely on you.

And when the banks got involved, things got worse. My credit was destroyed by years of failure. The banks weren't my friends   even a one-dollar overdraft was denied.

When I joked about it, they didn't laugh. When the business failed, they showed no mercy. Every opportunity they had to damage my credit further, they took it.

Still, I don't blame them. That's just business.

But no, I never did get that one-dollar overdraft.

The Addiction of Success

Looking back, I've realized something profound: chasing success is an addiction. It's intoxicating like a drug. There's no greater high than achieving a goal you've set your heart on. I believed that if I succeeded, everyone around me would benefit: my family, my friends. But I made one mistake I forgot to tell them about my grand plan. So, when everything fell apart, I was alone.

I destroyed my credit and exhausted myself chasing an illusion. But it wasn't a total loss, it was in fact a profound lesson. I was blinded by the bright lights of "success." My eyes were wide open but still shut.

The Manual of Life

Let me put it this way.

Imagine one evening, after a long day, you get home and collapse into bed, exhausted. You set your alarm for 5a.m wake up, and then place the "manual of life" on your nightstand, and drift off.

5a.m the alarm goes off. You reach for the manual and see that the pages are blank.

No instructions. No guidance. No plans for today or tomorrow only yesterday's pages filled in.

Panic sets in. You flip through the book still blank. Then a little voice inside your head says: "Maybe that's how life is."

And it's true. There's no manual for life not for me, not for you, not even for Jesus.

Each day, we wake up and write our own pages. We read the signs, make the choices, face the outcomes good or bad and try to do better tomorrow, it guess work. A shot in the dark with your eyes closed. It's much like throwing a lot of mud on the wall and hopefully some of it sticks.

And so, I kept going forward, filling out blank page after blank page.

So, should you.

Chapter 4

No Guarantee

Here's the big surprise: today or tomorrow isn't written down anywhere and no one has it all figured out, in spite of the experts and gurus. We all make it up as we go along.

Most of what we "discover" in life has been there all along, hiding in plain sight. It's only new to us. There's no manual to guide us. Every day, you and I wake up, glance back at yesterday, and realize we can't change a thing about it.

We dream of what could be and visualize what we want to be. And that's the beauty of life we get to construct today and even an opportunity to re-construct tomorrow.

Each day, we have the power to shape life into what we want. It's like grabbing that raging bull called life by the horns, wrestling it to the ground, and channelling its wild energy in our direction, it's very exciting. Or, we can stand aside, twiddling our thumbs, watching others do it.

It's really that simple. There are always signs along the way we just have to pay attention.

Sayings We Ignore

No Plan, No Path

I went into business without a plan; that's a sign a strong one that I was setting myself up for failure.

In a perfect world, we'd all have well-crafted plans that guarantee success. But this isn't a perfect world. Energy and enthusiasm will get you started, but not far. They'll get you out of bed but they won't keep you afloat.

Yes, I should have had a plan.

Unequal Partners,

Unequal Power

If your business partner doesn't contribute equal capital, that's a sign you're not equals.

Equality in partnerships is hard to achieve, but if it's possible, go for it. Every partner should invest equally: money, time, effort, and intellect. Most people want more than they put in. Many crave rewards but hate the work.

Also, if your partner brings their partner into the business without consulting you that's another sign. You're no longer equals. Sooner or later, they'll gang up and take control.

I've made that mistake. I entered partnerships without written agreements.

Lesson learned: put it in writing. Somewhere in the contract, it should clearly say

"This business is only between me and you" And remember: if your name isn't on the ownership documents, you're not the owner.

The Name on the Deed

Just because you're paying the mortgage doesn't mean you own the house. If your name isn't on the deed, you don't own it period.

Some people try to outsmart creditors or the government by putting property or companies in someone else's name. That's not smart it's surrender of rights. You're giving away control.

Don't make that mistake. Ownership must be visible and verifiable.

Don't Chase

Waterfalls

You can't swim down a waterfall. You'll crash, hit your head, and drown. Stay on solid ground.

When I first came to this country, young and full of energy, I went swimming at the community pool. The problem was I couldn't swim.

Yes, I know what you're thinking: "You were born on an island surrounded by ocean beaches!" that's true, but I never learned. I could dive and snorkel, sure, but real swimming? No. I avoided deep water like the plague.

Once, on a church trip to the lake, I was snorkelling, a frog darted across my face, I panicked in fair and nearly swallowed the entire lake. Lesson learned: don't swim if you can't swim.

Moral of the story don't get frightened easily, and if you must, snorkel in and learn to swim in your own bathtub first.

A Punch in the Nose Hurts

Play-fighting isn't play when the punches are real.

When I was younger me and my brothers and some friends, took up boxing. I lasted maybe three rounds or fights can't remember exactly but I remember the last one clearly. My opponent, was a friend of mine, he landed a clean punch right on my nose. It bled instantly. Seeing my own blood was enough. That was my cue to step out of the ring.

Lesson: don't pretend to be what you're not, know yourself, learn to fight properly, or stay out of the ring.

Wolves Don't Dance

When I was a kid, I went to the circus saw elephants stand tall on hind legs, tigers leap through rings of fire, and bears dance to the sound of drums. It was magical.

Later, while watching a TV documentary on wolves, I learned they don't dance and that they hunt in packs. They're intelligent, strategic, ruthless, and always hungry. I admired them.

Since then, I've believed this truth: don't try to dance with wolves. They're not there to entertain you. They're there to eat.

Being Depressed Is Depressing

I know what it feels like when life doesn't go as planned. I've seen it, felt it, and tasted it.

When I worked as a finance consultant, Fridays were the worst. That was deal-closing day payday. Those were the days when weeks of effort either paid off or collapsed.

If you're counting on one deal to cover your bills, and it falls through, well it's bone crushing. I have had that experience, the stress is suffocating. It zapped my breath away, I couldn't concentrate, my memory faltered; my motivation vanished. That was depression, even if I didn't call it that.

Sometimes it was exhaustion, sometimes fear, sometimes it was guilt. But the truth is that most of those feelings stemmed from chronic money problems. And yes, depression is real, and it's depressing.

Hope Is Not a Strategy

We wake up each day, trying to figure things out. The world spins. The sun shines. People do what people do.

Having hope is good but hope alone won't save you.

If you're driving to a city 500 miles away, you need a driver's license, a reliable car, gas money, and a plan. You can't "hope" your way there.

It's the same in life. If you have no clear plan, no career, no income, no stable relationships, hopelessness creeps in. To avoid that, build a strategy. Hope is not a plan, action is.

Exercise Is

Important

I've been blessed with good health most of my life so far, although gaining weight has always been a struggle. Still, I exercise and eat well, and I go to the gym regularly, get plenty of sleep; it keeps my mind and body aligned.

What baffles me is how many people go to the gym only to stare at their phones. How can you sweat if you're scrolling? Maybe, I missed that memo.

If your pants don't fit, if the climb up the stairs leave you breathless, if your scale groans when you step on, it's time. Get moving. Eat less and better. Sleep more.

Change your lifestyle, and you will change your life.

They Care (Maybe)

When I was out there, getting my butt kicked by life, sometimes all it took was that one phone call to remind me that someone cared.

My cousin Noel calls every day sometimes just for thirty seconds. My sister Lou calls every week from back home. Those moments ground me. They remind me of where I came from and even who I am.

And yes, sometimes I wonder if other people call just to spy or to steal time and my ideas, and get solutions on their problems. Maybe, but either way, it's nice to know someone's thinking and may listen to you.

Love Is Blooming

I've been in love or at least, I thought I was.

You will know that when she gets nervous around me or you, I took it as a sign. When she called often, I thought it meant something deeper. Then the wise man on the hill told me:

"You'll know she loves you when she leans toward you, when she touches you without invitation, when her eyes search for yours."

And yes, sometimes that affection comes with a pregnancy test and a baby nine months later. So maybe love was blooming or maybe something else was. Keep a open watch.

The Glove Doesn't Fit

Some relationships just don't fit no matter how hard you try.

The uneven yolk, you can be with the wrong person, just as you can be in the wrong place at the wrong time. And when that relationship produces children, you can't say it was all wrong, because something right came out of it. Still, sometimes, the glove just doesn't fit.

If it, that glove is too big, too small or too heavy, or if that relationship is too loud, too demanding, too this or too that or too much of something, stop, just stop struggling. Start anew, get new gloves.

The Phone Mystery

A Teaching Moment

I've been through heartbreak more than once. It's brutal. It tears through your chest, leaves you empty, angry, and confused.

There were days I couldn't get out of bed. Days I wanted to disappear. But in hindsight, heartbreak is one of life's greatest teachers.

It teaches you who you really are, how deeply you can love, how to forgive, and eventually how to recover and move on.

Heartbreak gives you the tools to rebuild yourself to grow emotionally and spiritually. Heart break is the fire that burnt away all illusions about love and life and leaves behind the truth.

And with that truth, that simple truth: you can survive anything, even the loss of love.

Reflection: No Guarantees, Only Growth

Life comes with no guarantees. The lessons, the heartbreaks, the wins, and the losses they all shape us. There's no map, no certainty, no written promise of success or happiness. But there are signs, and there is growth.

We may not know what tomorrow brings, but we do know one thing we're still here, still learning, and still strong enough to face the next round.

Even if it's the whale or the walk, the body keeps score.

Mine wrote a whole chapter without asking my permission.

One morning, I woke up and my legs said, "No." No explanation, no warning label, just a full stop. I tried to bargain "Just to the bathroom, just to the kitchen, just to the door" and my body replied, "Sit."

For a while, I thought it was fatigue. Then fear wore a groove into my ribs. When you've built your identity on hustle, stillness feels like a threat. The phone kept buzzing drivers, brokers, lenders, ghosts. I stared at it like it was a stranger.

That's when the story of Jonah came to mind and stopped being a Sunday School tale and became a street address. I wasn't flying anymore. I wasn't driving. I wasn't even walking. I was inside the whale, dark, quiet, and honest.

Inside that quiet I heard three things:

1. You've been sprinting through red lights.

2. You've been lifting things that weren't assigned to you.

3. You don't have to drown to learn to swim.

   So, I did what I hadn't done in years: I rested. I drank water like it was new. I walked to the corner and back. I noticed the way light moved across the wall. It sounds simple, even corny, but it was a miracle learning to live at walking speed.

Every day, I wrote one sentence in a notebook:

- "Walked to the mailbox."

- "Ate breakfast sitting down."

- "Called Noel and told him the truth."

That last one mattered. The truth wasn't pretty: I was scared, broke, and tired. He didn't fix it. He just listened. Sometimes listening is a rescue in plain clothes.

The whale eventually spat me out. Not onto a stage, not into a boardroom, onto a sidewalk. I took it as a sign. Life isn't a runway; it's a path. You don't take off; you just have to show up. You take just one step, then another; rinse and repeat.

And when I finally reached the park bench at the end of the block, I sat there like a king on a throne and said to myself; "We're walking this one" yes.

✓ The Unreturned Call

If you have to beg people to meet, partner, invest, or love you're negotiating with a "no."

Silence is a full sentence.

The Disappearing Weekend

If every Saturday looks like a Tuesday, you're not building you're burning. Rest is part of the work.

The All-Hands

Fire Drill

If every task is urgent, leadership is missing. Urgency is a spice, not a diet.

The Mystery Fee

If you can't explain a line item on your own budget, you're not ready to scale. Confusion compounds interest, too.

The Stomach

Whisper

Your gut is a board
member. If it keeps voting
"No,"
stop holding more
meetings.

The Closed Door

You Keep Kicking

Access is a teacher. If the door won't open, learn the hallway.

The Compliment

with a Leash

"Love what you're doing

if you must…"

If that "if" is a contract to

erase yourself.

Quickly decline with

thanks.

Chapter 5

Apprenticeships

I Didn't Know

I Had

I used to think mentors wore suits and scheduled coffee time. Turns out mine came disguised as problems, cashiers, and janitors.

- **Mr. Clarke, the building superintendent**, showed me how to coil a hose so it never knots. "Order saves your back," he said. I thought he was talking about water. He was talking about life.

- **A woman at the shipping yard:** clipped a bill of lading to my clipboard and said, "You don't move containers; you move information." I still think about that when stress tries to lift something heavier than it should.

- **The night-shift security guard**: taught me the arithmetic of dignity: eye contact + a name = a person. I learned that leadership starts with "Good evening, how's your night?"

Apprenticeship is sneaky. You sign up for wages, and you get wisdom by accident. I learned to be early. I learned to label the cable ends. I learned that a spare pen is a kind of insurance. And I learned that if you want the door guy to remember you, bring him coffee when nobody's watching.

One day, a young man asked me, "How do I find a mentor?" I told him the truth, I wish someone had told me:

"Do excellent small things near someone wise. They'll find you."

That's how I met Mrs. P, a client who ran a bakery like a symphony. She watched me fumble through a delivery, then handed me a warm loaf and said, "You're fast. Be precise." she wrote that on a sticky note which I kept. It saved me a thousand dollars in mistakes the next month.

Fast is easy. Precise is expensive at first and cheap forever.

Shop Notes
(Sayings I Keep Over the
desk in My head)

Measure Twice.

Breathe Once.

Then Cut.

Don't Raise Your Voice;

Raise your Standards.

If you Can't Trace it,

you Can't Trust it.

A "Favor"

that hurts your future

isn't a Favor.

Return the Cart, always.

Character has receipts.

Chapter 6

The Red Light

on the

Microphone

Back when I was young and loud, I sat behind a microphone and said the sentence that got me escorted out of a dream:

"Quit your job and start your own business—now."

I really meant "own your time." I meant "stop waiting for permission." What they heard was "set your life on fire by tomorrow morning."

The dean of the university and the radio station manager were polite, the way police lights are polite—blue and red, no discussion. I signed a paper and handed in my badge. My ego wanted to protest. My spirit wanted a pen. But, I just let it go, I had no control.

Losing that microphone taught me something precious: that volume is not conviction. The red light was a teacher. It told me to put craft behind courage. Since then, I've kept a simple checklist:

1. Is it true?

2. Is it kind?

3. Is it useful?

4. Is it mine to say?

5. Can I stand beside it in ten years?

If an idea passes those five, I'll say it on-air, on-paper, or on the sidewalk. If it fails, I'll write it in the journal and let it cool.

Here's what I would say now into that same microphone:

"If you have three months of expenses, one paying customer, and a plan you can explain to a 12-year-old, start the business. If not, start the plan."

It's less romantic. It's more loving.

Chapter 7

Glass House

Rules

I keep saying I live in a glass house. Here are the rules I've taped to the fridge:

- Don't throw stones.

Everybody's window is thin somewhere.

- Wash your own panes.

It's easy to see smudges on other people's lives. Keep some good glass cleaner for my own windows in stock.

- Let sunlight in.

Secrets grow mold. Open the blinds and name the mess.

- Replace what you break.

Apologize without a speech. Fix it if and where you can. Pay it back if and where you must.

The children know these rules. Some days I keep them well; some days I don't. When I fail, I try to fail toward the truth.

Once, after a hard week, I snapped at the cashier for moving slowly. My son watched the whole scene with those quiet eyes kids have. Back in the car, he said, "Dad, you were mean." I had no defense, like when lawyers appear. I turned the car around, with them in-tow, walked back in the store, and apologized; the cashier nodded. My son smiled. The glasshouse didn't crack that day.

The older I get, the more I believe this: Character is who cleans up.

Field Guide to Love

(3   Short Signs)

Signs its love:

You both protect each other's future in the present.

Sign its loneliness:

You negotiate your worth
by the hour.

Sign it's time to leave:

You need smaller dreams

to stay.

Chapter 8

WORK, MONEY, MERCY

I have been rich for ten minutes and broke for ten years. Money is loud when it enters and silent when it leaves. It has taught me mercy.

There was a time I judged people by their balance sheets—mine, theirs, the company's. Then life showed me a mother choosing between rent and insulin. Numbers folded into names. I started carrying gift cards in my wallet. Twenty dollars isn't salvation, but it's a sandwich and a bus ride, and sometimes that's the difference between despair and decision.

Mercy also looks like invoices sent on time, payment plans that honor dignity, and a "No" delivered before someone mortgaged their hope to your optimism. I used to say yes because I wanted to be liked. Now, I say yes when I can keep my promises.

A friend asked me, "How do you sleep with all those losses behind you?" I said, "On forgiveness." It isn't fancy. It's a warm blanket. I pull it over my shoulders and whisper, "I did what I could with what I knew. Tomorrow I'll know more."

Street-Proverbs

I Wish I Heard Sooner

If you can't explain it simply;

You're not ready to risk it

People don't flake; priorities do.

Believe the calendar.

The thing you avoid before noon is the thing ruining your month.

A plan with no dates is a wish; a plan with no margins is a trap

The bridge you burn tonight might be the only road home next winter

Chapter 9

The Small

Room

I used to dream in arenas. Now I pray for small rooms with the right people.

In a small room, you can hear a throat clear before a hard truth. You can see hands twitch when fear is driving. You can pass bread and mean it. That's how I want to build now—with the kitchen-table board meetings, with whiteboards and ugly handwriting, with laughter that doesn't check the time.

The small room is where I learned to father better—lecture less, be more present. Where I learned to be a son again—calling my sister, letting her fuss, saying "yes, I ate." It's where I learned to be a friend—showing up at moving day with duck tape and pizza, not just opinions.

If the universe offers me arenas again, I'll say thank you and walk in with a small-room heart. The mix is nice; the echo is dangerous.

Chapter 10

What the Signs

Say Today

- Build slow.

- Pay your debts in money and words.

- Tell the truth sooner.

- Walk every day.

- Hold your children without your phone in your hand.

- Stop at yellow lights; stop pretending they're green.

- Take provision seriously and yourself lightly.

- Pray like you're being listened to.

- Laugh when the soup boils over—then clean it.

- Write the page, even if it's just one line.

I still believe in second chances. I also believe in first choices—the ones you make in the quiet before the chaos. If you're reading this in a storm, there's a bench up ahead. Take a seat and a long breath. When you stand, walk, start slow, don't sprint, just walk. The road is patient. The signs are generous. And if you miss one today, there's another tomorrow.

We're not promised an easy map or life directions. We're promised a blank page.

Let's write the next line.

Chapter 11

Radio, Round Two

The second time I found a microphone, it wasn't in a studio.

It was a folding chair in a community center, a squeaky amp, and twenty people who wandered in because the poster said **Free Talk: Money, Work, and Meaning**.

No red light. No dean. No script. Just a circle of faces and a box of donuts and coffee. A man in a paint-splattered hood asked, "Should I quit my job?" Old me would've said it loud. New me asked, "Do you have three months of expenses and one paying customer?" He looked down at his boots and shook his head.

"Then build at walking speed," I said. "Keep the job. Start with one Saturday, then two and three. Find the first $100 that isn't from your boss. Bring the story back next month."

He did. He came back with photographs and a receipt book. The room clapped like church after a baptism. That's when I realized: I didn't need broadcast towers. I needed small rooms and true stories.

The show traveled—barbershops, basements, break rooms. The format was simple:

One lesson I learned the hard way.

One tool you can use by Friday.

One question you can only answer alone.

It wasn't radio. It was signal. And the frequency was humility.

What I Say Before Advice

Are you safe?

If not, fix that first.

Are you rested? Exhaustion makes bad math.

What problem are you solving—for whom?

Name them.

What will this cost you if it works?

Success has bills too.

Can you stand beside this in ten years?

If not, save your breath.

Chapter 12

Recovery from the Success High

I used to chase the spotlight like it was oxygen.

Now I look for the switch to turn some lights off.

Recovery didn't come with chips or medallions. It came with unglamorous habits:

- **I learned to budget time like money.** If I overspend an hour on nonsense, something worthy goes into debt.
- **I stopped calling chaos "momentum."** Busy isn't brave.
- **I kept promises to myself that nobody could see.** Bed made, shoes by the door, water first.

Withdrawal is real. When you step away from adrenaline, silence feels itchy. You want a new crisis to scratch it. I started noticing the itch and naming it out loud: "That's my old addiction talking." Naming it took half its power.

I also wrote a different scoreboard:

- Did I tell the truth sooner today?
- Did I choose a walk over a worry?
- Did I do one thing my future self will thank me for?

When I slip (and I do), I don't binge on shame. I reset. Recovery is laps, not a finish line.

The "Enough" Test

Get Enough sleep to be kind?

Make Enough money to pay on time?

Give Enough margin to help a friend?

Show Enough humility to ask for help?

Have Enough faith to try again?

If I could've say yes to three, the day is livable. Four is grace. All five, that's wealth.

Chapter 13

Father on a Tuesday

Grand gestures are easy. Tuesdays are hard.

My kids don't remember the speeches. They remember:

- the time I burned pancakes and we ate them anyway,
- the apology I gave a cashier with them watching,
- the way I put the phone face down during their stories.

I once tried to fix everything in a weekend—discipline, homework, room cleaning, life plan. It lasted two days. Then I learned the quieter math of fatherhood:

- **Attention = Love.** Ten focused minutes beats an hour of distracted presence.
- **Rituals > Resolutions.** Walk after dinner. Read before bed. Saturday morning calls to family.
- **Repair is the win.** We will mess up. We will make amends.

One night a few years back, my daughter asked, "Dad, are we rich?" I said, "In some ways." She frowned. "What ways?" I pointed to the table—dented, sticky, surrounded by us. "This way."

We're not perfect. Here is a hug with love, We're together. On Tuesdays, that's gold.

Signs You Owe an Apology

You're rehearsing a defense no one asked for.

You're avoiding a store, a street, or a face.

Your child starts whispering when your name comes up.

Your sleep keeps stopping at 3a.m.

The story makes you the hero and the victim.

Say "I'm sorry,"

not

"I'm sorry, but."

Then ask,

"How can I re

pair this?"

Chapter 14

Business as a

Blessing

And

Boundary

I still believe in business. I just don't believe it's supposed to eat me.

Here's my new covenant with work:

- **No idols.** If the enterprise asks me to trade relationships for revenue, the answer is no.
- **Clarity first.** If I can't draw the model on one page with arrows a child can follow, I'm not ready.
- **Cash is oxygen.** Track it daily. Breathe on purpose.
- **People over performance, performance over promises.** Hire character, measure outcomes, ignore hype.
- **Exit early.** If the numbers or the values turn against us, we leave before smoke becomes fire.

I keep a "why now" paragraph taped inside my notebook. It reminds me who this is for and what a good week looks like. When offers arrive dressed like opportunities but smell like distraction, I read the paragraph out loud. If it doesn't harmonize, I pass.

A younger me thought saying **yes** was courage.

Current me knows saying **no** builds a future.

Tools I Actually Use

A paper calendar where

wins and worries share

space.

Envelopes labeled Rent,

Food, Debt, and Fun.

Old School cash sorting,

for clarity.

A "call list" of one, three or five people I check on every week

(and who check on me).

A 20-minute timer for the task I'm avoiding.

When it dings, I decide:

Continue or Consciously Defer.

A walk. Always a walk.

Chapter 15

Grief's Quiet Classroom

Loss doesn't shout. It rearranges furniture.

I've lost people who built my bones and named my days—my father, my mother, my grandmother. Grief made the house echo I live in. For a time I tried to outwork the silence. It followed me to every job site and boardroom. Finally I let it sit beside me.

Grief taught me to bless the ordinary:

- the smell of soap on a line of shirts.
- the sound of keys on a table by the door.
- The way someone says my name when they're not rushing.

On their birthdays, I make the food they loved. On mine, I call the people they would have scolded me for forgetting. I keep a small altar of receipts and photos: proof that love happened here. I try to.

If you're grieving, here's the sign I wish I'd seen sooner: **Nothing is wrong with you for carrying love in a heavier form.** Carry it, then, rest. Carry it again. Then, carry on.

Street Prayer

Be God of the small room and the long road,

teach me to see the next right turn, and the right step.

To tell the truth before it festers,

To choose people over the applause.

To work like a craftsman and rest like a child.

How to keep my house that is made of glass and grace, crack free.

Amen.

Chapter 16

The Phone,
The Silence,
The Start

There's a mystery I still don't fully understand: the phone that doesn't ring when you need it to, and won't stop when you don't want it to. I used to chase it, worship it, now I almost hate it.

Instead, now I treat it like a tool. I have hours when it sleeps in a drawer. During those hours, I write one page—just one, maybe two. Sometimes it's a sentence and even a paragraph: **"We're still here."** Sometimes it's a plan: three boxes with arrows that make sense. Sometimes it's a memory I don't want to lose.

That small practice—one page—has rescued more of my life than any grand strategy.

People ask, "What's the first step?"

Here it is, the one I give to the guy wearing the paint-splattered hoodie and the night-shift nurses and fathers on a Tuesday:

- Write down the smallest honest next action.
- Do it before the next noon.
- Tell one person you did it, something, whatever it is.
- Just wash, rinse and repeat tomorrow.

That's it. That's the sign. That's the path. That's the book you're holding.

We don't get guarantees. We do get mornings and that is enough to begin again.

Signs

What do I mean when I say "signs"?

We're all busy—some of us moving on purpose, some of us drifting. Either way, the universe keeps dropping hints: turn left on green arrow only, slow down, run, stop, and go now. Those are signs.

They're everywhere—on walls, in cars, at home, at work, inside our relationships. Most of the time we ignore them, then, when life unravels, we cry, complain, announce what good people we are, and ask God, "Why me?"

But God—the universe—usually showed us the signs long before we messed things up. The writing is and was on the wall. Call it a spider sense in the back of the mind, a tug in the gut. Some of us don't know how to read it, some forgot how, others refuse to look.

Often, there are many signs that things aren't what they should be.

Signs in Love

Cheating—how do we know?

When the cell phone suddenly has a pass code. When conversations end the moment you walk in. When more time is spent on that phone than with you. When the talking fades, the patience runs thin, and the words start to belittle. When late nights at "work" multiply and touch disappears—even in bed. When the car sits in the driveway while they finish a call before coming inside.

Another sign: gambling away the savings. That's addiction and a warning flaring red sign. Money can't be trusted in those hands until the sickness is faced.

And when your partner vacations without you for no good reason— that's not "space." It's a search.

I missed the signs once. They led me to divorce court. It broke my heart. It will break yours too.

More Trouble

Motorbikes have two wheels and one chance. I've stood at bedsides and at funerals after crashes. People choose what they choose; it's a free world—mostly.

Once in Montréal, friends and I rode to the island's highest point and flew downhill like kids do, free of consequences. Mid decent, my friend's handle bar popped clean off at forty miles an hour.

For a second, it seemed funny; then he hit the ground, hard. We were still laughing many minutes later, even as we patched him up with band aids. He didn't laugh. That moment cracked our friendship. We eventually stopped talking and later learned he moved across the country. Years later, I heard he died, killed in a fist fight; I never got to apologize face to face, only silently.

Sign: if the handlebar pops off while you're bombing a hill, a crash is coming. Also: don't find joy in a friend's pain.

Another time, I watched a wheel pass my car on the highway. News flash: the car didn't turn into a tricycle. Pull over. You're about to crash.

Friendship Requires Maintenance

Real friendship takes management. I'm blessed with a few good ones—it took work and take constant management.

Once, a friend wired money without me asking, when I was down to my last dollar. A friend picked me up at 3 a.m. in winter when the car died. A true friend offered the couch when I needed a place to land. And yes, the unpaid therapy sessions—the wisdom that kept me standing.

Sign you don't have a real friend: If the friend kicks you out of the car because you can't pay for gas while crossing the country. Get one real friend.

Signs of Coming Trouble (Business)

One winter, I reached my restaurant to find the locks changed and an eviction notice taped inside the glass. My first feeling was grief, for the team and the loss. My second was a sense of relief. The landlord mercifully had cut the ball and the chain from my neck.

The signs were always there: the bounced checks, the overdue bills stuffed in drawers. The many calls I didn't want to take or return. When rent or mortgage goes unpaid and the notices that showed up, the end has arrived. If you're sleeping in a car or under a bridge, you're homeless—or intoxicated by something that's killing you. Read the signs earlier if you can.

Don't Be Lost

I started my first business in Montréal with zero experience in the industry. I wasn't lost, despite that fact, I knew where I wanted to go, to the top. There were days I stood in unfamiliar places facing overwhelming problems—but I still knew my direction. I tell my kids: there are many roads to get to any one place. Pick one and head there.

One afternoon I couldn't find my car in a mall lot. For a minute I wondered if it was towed, stolen—or if I'd imagined owning a car at all. But no, I'd just forgotten the spot. Here's what I know: if you know where you want to go, you're not lost. Look for the signs.

Don't Be a Fool

There's a story about trading a cow for magic beans. My grandmother—God rest her soul—had her own version: *you can tell a lot about a man by the company he keeps.* She was right.

When I went to town as a boy, I saw men lingering on corners, whistling at girls and wasting time. I thought they were cool, but I later realized that they were lawless time wasters'. She said if you lay down with dogs, and you get fleas—or at least smell like the dog.

My father had rules too: no hanging on corners he said. People will judge you by your company. Spend time with drunks and the unproductive, and you'll be counted as one.

Sign: fools keep company with fools. Don't take advice from them. Seek the people who add value to your life—who push you toward wisdom.

And a personal rule: i have found that the longer I'm alone, the wiser and more peaceful I had become.

During my hardest seasons, the matinee saved me. Friday afternoons, I hid in a dark theater while the world burned down. A friend would sometimes drive to a nearby city and hide in a hotel all weekend. I took solo road trips—city to city, just me and the highway. Therapy on wheels. Those escapes kept me from exploding. Alone time gave me my best ideas—and made me bearable to myself.

Yesterday Is Forever; Work the Now

They say if you don't know where you're from, you don't know who you are. They also say if you forget the past, you'll repeat it. Both can be true.

But here's today's assignment: you can't change yesterday. Work the now.

Don't Jump Out of a Plane

A pilot friend told me: birds fly by nature; humans fly in metal tubes full of controlled explosions, it's miracles with seat-belts. They make the strong people sit near the exits to help others in emergencies.

If you jump from that plane without a parachute, you'll meet the ground fast. That's a sign. If you're going to jump from that plane, make sure you have a working parachute

If you arrive late to work after repeated warnings? That's a sign too—that you are going to be fired, soon. Don't be a late bird.

Hair, Humor, and Acceptance

I had and wore loc's for years. I never saw a barber. A guy in my office had a new comb-over daily—you know, male pattern baldness in denial. We joked at the water cooler about it. I finally told him: *everyone can see it—own it.* Then, he wanted implants, (hair plug in's). I thought it's his head, it's his choice.

One day, I touched my scalp and felt smoothness…air. I wasn't going to let the hair commercials convince me to transplant my leg hair to my head. My brain might grow a knee up there. Instead, I chose acceptance. If I couldn't grow more hair, I'd grow more courage.

Too Sweet, Too Still

In the West, we have refrigerators full of options. Science says thirst can masquerade as hunger, and we eat when we should drink. So we overdo sugar, starch, alcohol, couches, and screens—and under do movement and sleep.

People don't want to hear it until a health crisis shouts it. You can wait for a doctor to read your lab results—or you can read the mirror, the tight waistline, the breathlessness going up and down the stairs, the groaning scale. Ask the person you live and love, chances are they will be honest and tell you the truth. They can see the signs.

So, change your habits, you will change your life.

Don't Hide From the Truth

We confuse truth with rudeness because truth sometimes stings. Tell someone they're too loud, dishonest, or neglecting hygiene—you'll meet resistance. But denial doesn't change reality. It just delays repair.

In business, I missed obvious danger signs: poor planning, bad money management, and a refusal to face facts. Stressed and distracted, I ignored the blinking red light that read **BROKE**. Ironically, the day I finally admitted I was broke was the day I began to fix it. Truth first, plans after.

Also, if the boss makes the rules, know your position. If it's pitch-black outside, it's either night or a storm. Read the sky.

Know Where You Are (and where and Who You're Not).

I ran a nightclub while working days at my brokerage. Eighteen hour stretches for months. Fatigue chained me to the floor. I napped in parking lots on the way home.

Once I fell asleep at a red light and woke to a taxi driver knocking on my window: "You okay, bud?" Another time, I passed out in a lot at 3am I eventually woke to Chinese voices and signs everywhere. For a second, I thought I'd teleported to Beijing, China. but no—it was just Chinatown, downtown Toronto.

Then there was the morning I woke beside a beautiful woman who called me "husband," and I couldn't remember a wedding. Reality check: I had consumed too many alcoholic drinks, and it was a dream I couldn't afford.

Know where you are. Know who you're not.

Sleep Matters

Up at 3 a.m., wide awake since midnight? You're likely stressed, over stimulated, or overworked. Chronically poor sleep bends our emotions and invites anxiety and depression which then breaks our sleep even more. Rest is medicine. Get some.

Thunder, Fire, and Hammers

if you hear thunder? Lightning already happened. If rain is pouring through your ceiling, that's not "a vibe." It's a hole in the roof. Call a roofer.

See smoke? There's fire. If the fire department is kicking your door because dinner became a disaster, accept the sign: you're not a chef—yet. Turn off the stove, go with the fire people.

if you smash your finger with a hammer or shoot a nail through your boot? You're not a carpenter. Call one. Stay whole.

Time's Knock, Sports' Limits

That loud sound isn't just a punch to the head—it's time reminding you you're getting older. Athletes get hurt because they push limits. Weekend warriors forget they have limits, too.

In my forties, I played pickup ball with my teenage son and his friends. I was cooking—until I heard a bang and a snap that no one else heard. I turned to see who kicked me. No one did, the next step I took lead to my collapsed. I had ruptured my Achilles. What followed was months of crutches, a year to walk and jog right again.

Sign: know and respect your stage of life. Leave the sky walking and dunking to the twenty-year-olds.

Knife Fight

I'm five foot and nine inches tall, and a lean 160 pounds. I'm not fighting a bouncer twice my size. In grade school I lost a fistfight and my one of my older cousins rescued me. Most of my later fights were mental and financial. But when someone brought a knife, I brought a bat. I don't want to gett cut.

Bring a knife to a gunfight and you get shot—or laughed out of town. Also, I once tried to ride a horse that clearly didn't want me on it. I forced it. The horse threw me. The hip still hurts and complains. Respect wild things and wild people.

Keep Cash in the Pocket(s)

ATMs fail. Networks go down. Banks freeze accounts. I've had deposits swallowed by the taxman the same day. I've stood at a gas station with a declined card and an empty wallet. That's a sign you'll be washing dishes if you just ordered the lobster.

Carry a little cash. It's not old fashioned; it's insurance.

Don't Cry Over Spoiled Milk (or Eggs)

The saying is "don't cry over spilled milk," but here's my remix: if the eggs have hatched into chicks while in your fridge, your fridge is finished. Get a new one. Some problems need a reset, not a speech.

The Fuel Light Doesn't Negotiate

When the low fuel light comes on, you can't argue with it. Head to the nearest gas station. Hope won't fuel or move the car.

Create Your Own Image

"Image is everything," so they say. Dress well; first impressions matter. But deeper: if we're made in God's image, we're made to create. So create your own reality—honestly, consistently, with love.

Book II

Mustafa Tut Brown

Chapter 1

The First Gasp

of Air

Someone told me life is mostly pain and suffering, with only a few drops of joy. I know it's true. Calling life "hard" is polite.

It starts with birth. That first breath burns—the lungs scream—and you cry. Not because the doctor taps you, but because your spirit just arrived and declared, I want to live.

At first, you are helpless and adored. Needs met. Language taught. Love delivered. Bless those who poured into you.

Then come the waves—punches you don't see, curveballs you can't hit yet. One day, you discover a new word: job. You'll resist. You'll delay. You'll invent excuses. You're used to other people feeding and clothing you, cleaning up your mess. But the gravy train ends and life begins.

Self-reliance will show up with its lunch pail in hand. Mom and Dad can't do this part for you.

Chapter 2

Education

Education is vital—formal and informal. When I started, I had no idea what I was doing. In college I felt very lost. The classroom that taught me the most wasn't state-funded. It was the University of Hard Knocks—core subjects: pain and suffering, success and failure.

From birth, people have been doing things for us—cooking, cleaning, homework, "free passes" handed out for charm or family name. That season ends. Now it's your turn.

You'll need to cook and clean, earn a living, build a career or a business, choose your friends, your clothes, your taste, your address and your lifestyle. Odds are you'll get it wrong more than once. Good news: you'll get chances to try again.

When the dust settles, reinvention knocks. That's when your real education begins. Enroll yourself. Be brave. Dive in. The pressure is on you now.

I cleaned up and tightened your whole draft (the "Signs" section and everything that followed) for clarity, tone, and flow—keeping your voice but smoothing grammar, repetition, and pacing. It's all in the canvas to the right.

Chapter 3

Relationships:

Built, Not

Found

Success in any relationship looks less like magic and more like management. Not cold spreadsheets—warm, daily attention. Think of it as a living venture with shared values, clear roles, and regular audits of care.

Our First Relationship

Before we meet the world, we meet appetite. Food is the first covenant: cry → comfort. Then come blankets, toys, and the smell of a warm bed. We learn love and territory at the same time—what is mine, what I'll share, what I'll defend. And standing at the gate of all this goodness is Mom. No mom, no milk. No milk, no peace. Naturally, our earliest map of trust is drawn around her name.

Then life adds new covenants—work, friends, money. Each one asks the same questions: Will you show up? Will you tell the truth? Will you carry your part?

Marriage Is a Venture (With a Soul)

People don't like hearing that marriage is "like a business," but the parts that fail often fail for business reasons: unclear expectations, fuzzy budgets, silent resentment, and a partner who feels like an unpaid employee.

So I think of marriage this way:

- Mission: Why are we together beyond chemistry? What future are we building?

- Roles: Who holds which keys? Not fixed by gender—set by strengths.
- Governance: How do we decide, disagree, and repair?
- Cashflow of Care: Time, attention, affection—deposits and withdrawals we both can see.

Hearts lead us in; habits keep us in. The old saying from back home—"come see me and come live with me are two different things"—is a whole university course. Living under one roof reveals the raw data: quirks, rhythms, old wounds. That's when we choose: do we build, or do we bail?

Changing Roles, Same Promise

Once upon a time, the blueprint was simple: one breadwinner, one homemaker. Now the roles braid and bend. Some women carry the larger paycheck. Some men run the home front. The promise remains: we protect each other's future. If kids arrive (and they often do), the complexity multiplies. Sleep shrinks. Chores expand. Romance becomes logistics with candles.

Many couples feel a drop in happiness in the early kid years. It isn't failure—it's friction. The answer isn't blame; it's design. Calendars become sacred. Ten-minute check-ins matter. And repair becomes the love language after the kids are asleep.

Signs Your Relationship Needs Maintenance

The phone feels safer than your partner.

Logistics has replaced laughter for more than a season.

You're keeping score instead of keeping promises.

Money talks only happen in emergencies.

Apologies come with closing arguments.

What Helps (From My Scar Tissue)

Weekly stand-up: 20 minutes, two questions: What worked? What hurts?

Transparent money: One page, all bills, both eyes.

Rituals: Walks after dinner. Screens off in bed. Hug at the door.

Repair first: We can debate the dishes after we mend the tone.

Exit ramps for anger: A phrase that means pause—"I want us, give me ten."

Love is poetry. Marriage is also punctuation. Put the commas where you can breathe.

Chapter 4

Adversity: The Letter and the Forge

Adult life is heavy. Decisions stack like cinder blocks. Some days, the floor tilts and you swear gravity changed. Friends are busy. Family loves you, but can't carry you. Bills multiply. The room gets loud.

I've known that free fall feeling: legs unsteady, head buzzing, options thin. When I finally looked up from my own storm, I saw the same rain falling on everyone else. Nobody escapes the weather.

The Dear John Letter

One day, the door opens to an emptied room. The couch is gone. The frames are missing. On the counter sits a note:

"Dear John… this isn't working. The ship is sinking. I can't do this anymore."

If it hasn't happened to you, it might. If it has, you remember the exact weight of that paper. Evictions, layoffs, repossessions—they share a font. You'll ask all the good questions: Why me? I paid my taxes, I helped my neighbors, I kept my vows. The universe won't hold a press conference.

It will, however, replay the signs you missed: the late fees you called glitches, the silences you called rest, the cracks you painted over. I've been there.

What Adversity Actually Does

It exposes structure. It burns away slogans. It forges or fractures.

Mine has done both—broke me open and then rebuilt what mattered.

When help doesn't arrive, it isn't always betrayal. Sometimes it's reality: other people are in their own storms. That's when you learn the difference between loneliness and solitude. Loneliness begs. Solitude builds.

Field Guide: First 72 Hours After Impact

- Stabilize: Eat, shower, sleep. Your brain needs glucose and rest more than it needs a manifesto.
- Inventory: What's true today—cash on hand, debts due, safe places to sleep, three people you can call.
- Triage: Stop the leaks—cancel auto payments you can't cover, return what you can't afford, talk to the landlord before the lock changes.
- Communicate clean: "Here's what happened. Here's what I'm doing. Here's what I need." No novels, no blame.
- Small win: One task finished before noon. Momentum is medicine.

Signs You're Getting Stronger (Even If It Still Hurts)

You tell the truth without a performance.

You sleep six hours in a row.

You ask for help without apologizing for existing.

You can list what you control and what you don't.

You can laugh without pretending everything's fine.

Adversity will visit. When it knocks again—and it will—I plan to answer with a cleaner house: fewer illusions, clearer ledgers, stronger rituals of love. A forge is hot, but it makes good metal.

Chapter 5

Money, Trust, and Repair

Money doesn't just buy things; it reveals things. It shows priorities, fears, habits, and hidden wounds. I used to think money problems were about math. Now I know they're about meaning.

The Mirror Called Money

Every relationship has a mirror moment when the bills hit the table. It's not about who earns more—it's about how each of you defines safety. To one person, safety means a cushion in the bank. To another, it means freedom to spend without permission. Those differences, unspoken, can kill intimacy faster than infidelity.

When I had money, I used it to prove my worth. When I lost money, I thought I'd lost my worth. Both were lies. The truth is, money only magnifies what's already there: generosity or fear, stewardship or ego.

The Practice of Financial Honesty

I learned a ritual that saved both relationships and sanity:

1. Open the numbers. Show the real accounts—the balances, debts, and upcoming bills.
2. Name the emotions. Fear, guilt, resentment—say them aloud. You can't budget what you hide.
3. Assign roles. Who tracks, who pays, who checks receipts—not forever, just for now.
4. Review weekly. Ten minutes, Friday night. Celebrate little

progress.

Money fights often aren't about dollars. They're about power and trust. When one person hides spending or saving, it's usually a symptom of deeper anxiety, control, pride, or survival fear. Healing starts with acknowledgment: I'm scared, not selfish.

Lessons From the Fall

When creditors called daily, I stopped answering. That silence cost me more than interest—it cost me dignity. Once I picked up the phone and spoke honestly, solutions appeared: payment plans, forgiveness, and advice. Most institutions respond better to truth than to avoidance.

Sign: You're healing financially when you can open the bills without your pulse racing.

The fix isn't quick. But honesty compounds faster than interest ever could.

Money Rules I Live By

If you can't pay cash, ask twice: Do I need this or want this?

Keep one small fund labeled "mercy." It's for helping someone else.

Celebrate paying off a debt more than buying something new.

Audit subscriptions; loyalty is expensive.

Give, even when it pinches—it keeps greed on a leash.

Chapter 6

Faith, Forgiveness, and Forward Motion

I've tried to outrun faith and found it waiting at every detour. Not religion, necessarily—faith. The quiet conviction that tomorrow can be better if I move with honesty today.

The Silence Between Storms

After failure or heartbreak, there's a numb season. You clean, walk, cook, scroll, but inside it's just wind. That silence is not punishment; it's preparation. The soul resets in the quiet.

One dawn, I prayed without formality: "If there's still a purpose for me, show it." The answer didn't come in thunder—it came in phone calls, job offers, and one kind stranger who said, "You look tired. Take a seat."

Faith doesn't erase pain; it reframes it. It says, this weight builds muscle.

Forgiveness: The Hardest Math

I've held grudges like investments, expecting interest. All I earned was exhaustion. Forgiveness is emotional bankruptcy court—you declare the debt uncollectible so you can rebuild.

Sometimes you forgive others. Sometimes you forgive yourself for staying too long, believing too hard, or spending what you didn't have. Either way, it's a release, not a verdict.

I once met a pastor who said, "Unforgiveness is like holding your breath to punish someone who's already gone." That line stuck. I started breathing again.

Forward Motion

Forgiveness clears the runway. Forward motion is the takeoff.

Start small: clean the room, answer the email, take a walk, write the thank-you note. Progress is sacred, even when invisible.

When I finally forgave the people who hurt me—and the man in the mirror—I noticed something surprising: peace felt lighter than blame. I could finally see the signs again.

Signs of Renewal

You wake up with one plan instead of ten regrets.

You can bless the past without wanting it back.

You feel gratitude

before caffeine.

You say "no" without guilt.

You pray not for escape, but for endurance.

Faith, forgiveness, and forward motion—three tools I never leave home without. They don't make life easy, but they make it meaningful.

Chapter 7

Diversity

Over the years, I've found myself in all kinds of predicaments — in business, personal life, finances, and even legal troubles. Each situation forced me to draw on the many experiences and ideas collected in my mind. I had to problem-solve from memory, from what I'd learned through trial and error, and sometimes from the wisdom of others who had walked similar paths.

Every one of those challenges tested my core. To endure them, I had to recognize something crucial — resilience is diversity in action. It's the ability to think differently, to adapt, to be flexible, and to use every tool in your box, even the unconventional ones. Sometimes you have to see through walls, using what I call "x-ray vision" — the ability to look beyond the surface and identify your unique point of difference.

Diversity isn't just about people or culture. It's about mindset — the capacity to hold multiple ideas at once, to listen deeply to perspectives that differ from your own, and to remain open to being wrong. It's the skill of reinventing your thinking each time life knocks you down. Those who master this survive. Those who don't stagnate.

Chapter 8

Creativity

When life corners you, get creative. Look for solutions in places you wouldn't normally look. Call the person you stopped talking to. Revisit old friends, call on forgotten skills, and hidden passions. Creativity lives in the spaces we often ignore.

I remember a time when I was in deep financial trouble. My partner had left, my business was collapsing, and I sat in the basement, blank and defeated. Then the phone rang. A friend called just to check in. As I explained my situation, he paused and said, "Why don't you just refinance the property?"

It was so simple, yet I couldn't see it. Stress and fear had strangled my creativity. That one suggestion changed everything. I realized that pressure kills imagination faster than failure ever could. I needed every ounce of creative energy to rebuild my life, to design new ventures, and to re-create myself. Each time I started over, I had to introduce a new version of me — someone wiser, sharper, and more valuable to the world. Creativity became my lifeline. It wasn't just about art or innovation; it was survival. Every product, service, idea, and even the jokes I told were part of that creative reinvention. The truth is simple: when you stop creating, you start decaying. Your value — in work, relationships, and self — depends on your ability to imagine better ways forward.

Be creative, or be replaced.

Creativity isn't a luxury. It's the currency of survival.

Chapter 9

Motivation

Motivation — it's the engine behind every action, the invisible force that moves you from intention to impact. The word comes from "motive," meaning need, desire, or drive. It's the psychological energy that fuels our behavior toward goals.

You don't need an alarm clock when you're truly motivated. Motivation wakes you. It keeps you moving when others quit. It's the difference between dreamers and doers, between those who start and those who finish. Some say success belongs to the strongest. I say it belongs to the most consistent — those who keep moving when strength fades. Motivation is not a mood; it's a mindset. You can train it like a muscle, feeding it with discipline, belief, and repetition. Think of it this way: everyone can run, but only the one who wakes earlier, trains harder, and endures longer reaches the finish line. You have to want it — more than comfort, more than sleep, more than fear.

Motivation is in you, buried like gold. You dig it out through purpose, persistence, and pain. It drives you to overcome losses and failures, to minimize suffering, and to maximize growth and reward. It's what gets you up after rejection, heartbreak, or defeat.

Remember: motivation is not wishful thinking. It's not optimism. It's motion. It's what you do when no one's watching — when the cheering stops, and it's just you and your willpower. As the great athlete once said, "It's not the shoes. It's you. Just do it."

Chapter 10

Spirituality

Spirituality is personal — a path only you can define. It's the quiet foundation beneath purpose and the energy that shapes everything above it. It's a belief in something greater, whether that's God, the universe, nature, or the collective memory of our ancestors.

Over time, I discovered that spirituality wasn't a distant theory. It was the breath between thoughts — the awareness that guided me when everything else fell apart. I had to surrender to what I call the "natural mystic," that unseen rhythm moving through life. The more I tried to control outcomes, the more chaos followed. Only when I stopped, listened, and paid attention did the signs become clear.

Spirituality, for me, meant resetting — cutting out distractions, television, noise, even people who drained my energy. It meant asking, What really matters? It meant reconnecting with the divine within — that spark of creation that lets us imagine, heal, and rebuild.

True spirituality isn't about rituals alone. It's about connection — with yourself, with others, with the natural and cosmic forces that sustain life. It's about tuning into the same frequency as creation itself.

Meditation, prayer, reflection — these are not chores but channels. They align your mind, body, and soul. They help you hear the whisper beneath the noise.

Spirituality gives meaning to struggle. It teaches that pain isn't punishment — it's preparation. It connects us to the infinite cycle of life, death, and rebirth.

African Spirituality

According to ancient African and Egyptian traditions, spirituality is woven into every part of life. It isn't confined to temples or scriptures but lives in stories, songs, festivals, and the wisdom of elders. It honors both the visible and the invisible — ancestors, spirits, nature, and the supreme creator.

In many African beliefs, every living being, object, and place carries spiritual essence. Humanity's role is to balance, maintaining harmony with the creator and the natural world. Life and death are seen as transitions, not endings. Ancestors continue to influence the living, guiding and protecting those who remember them.

Traditional African spirituality recognizes multiple gods and intermediaries, yet all flow from one divine source. It values community, reverence for life, and respect for unseen forces. Healing, medicine, and spirituality are one and the same — restoring not just the body, but the spirit.

Before the arrival of major world religions, these beliefs formed the foundation of culture, morality, and science across the continent. Even now, echoes of those truths remain — the drumbeat of the ancestors still vibrates beneath our modern noise.

Spirituality, in all its forms, reminds us: we are not separate from creation. We are a living part of it.

Chapter 11

Spirituality And Its Use

From the dawn of human existence, spirituality has been understood as a path toward a higher state of awareness — the perfection of one's being, the pursuit of wisdom, and communion with the Creator. Across cultures, it has always been about reaching beyond the material toward something timeless and divine.

Spirituality often includes practices such as meditation, prayer, fasting, study of sacred texts, and following a trusted guide or teacher. But above all, it begins with supreme love — love of the Divine, and love of self. Without self-love, the climb toward enlightenment becomes impossible.

As the Indian spiritual teacher Meher Baba wrote:

"The spiritual path is like climbing to the mountain top through hills and valleys and thorny woods, along steep and dangerous precipices.

If there is one thing most necessary for ultimate success and safe arrival at the top, it is love — love of self and life. All other qualities will come if you faithfully follow the whispers of the unerring guide of love."

The Foundation: Love of Self

Self-love is not vanity. It's the deep appreciation for who you are — body, mind, and spirit. It grows through conscious actions that nourish your whole being. Without it, success becomes a moving target that can never be caught. With it, you build the resilience to thrive.

Practical Steps to Nurture Spirituality

1. Stop Comparing Yourself to Others

We live in a competitive world, but comparison is poison to the spirit. You are a one-of-one — no one has your path, your scars, your soul.

Focus on your own journey; redirect that energy toward your growth. Freedom follows.

2. Release Others' Opinions

People's expectations can imprison you if you let them. You can't please everyone — and you're not supposed to.

Let go of worry; it slows your evolution. Live in alignment, not approval.

3. Embrace Failure — and the Fear of It

We're told "nobody's perfect," but few truly believe it. Failure is not the enemy; it's the teacher.

Give yourself permission to make mistakes, to fall, to start again. The more you do, the stronger you become.

4. Care for the Body That Carries You

Your body is sacred — the vessel of your spirit. Its worth isn't in appearance, but in performance and vitality.

Exercise, eat clean, rest, stretch, laugh often. Move with gratitude. The body you care for will carry your dreams further.

5. Remove Toxic People and Environments

Protect your energy. Some people bring storms wherever they go, like a hurricane or a winter storm— let them pass.

It's not cruel to detach from negativity; it's wise. Freedom begins when you stop apologizing for choosing peace.

6. Process Fear — Don't Run From It

Fear is a signal, not a sentence. Listen to it.

When you confront your fears, you uncover their true message — often about what you value most. Facing fear is how you reclaim clarity and peace.

7. Trust Yourself

You already know what's right for you. Your intuition is your oldest compass.

When you start trusting your judgment, you'll make better decisions and find greater calm in the process.

8. Create and Seize Opportunities

There's no perfect moment to act. The time is now.

Life rarely hands out ideal circumstances — but it rewards courage. Step into the unknown, and doors will open.

9. Put Yourself First

You're the driver of your own life. Caring for yourself isn't selfish — it's essential.

Take breaks, move your body, dance, rest, or just breathe. "Me time" is not indulgence; it's maintenance for your spirit.

10. Accept That Pain Is Temporary

Pain, fear, and joy are all passing guests. Feel them, learn from them, but don't let them define you.

Understanding emotion gives you empathy — and empathy deepens your spiritual maturity.

11. Be Bold and Speak Your Truth

Boldness is spiritual strength in motion. Use your voice — it matters.

Don't wait for permission. Start the conversation. Confidence grows with every truth spoken.

12. Observe the Beauty Around You

Notice at least one beautiful thing every day — rain on the window, a laugh, a sunset.

Gratitude turns ordinary moments into sacred ones. It lifts the spirit and opens the heart.

13. Be Kind to Yourself

The world can be loud and cruel. Don't add your voice to that chorus.

Speak kindly to yourself. Celebrate how far you've come, not how far you have left to go. Joy is an act of resistance.

The Takeaway

Even when you don't feel powerful, remember what you've survived — the nights you thought would never end but did, the pain you thought would break you but didn't. You're still here, alive and capable of becoming more than you imagined.

Be patient with yourself. Self-love and spiritual growth take time. But they will take root, and when they do, they'll feed every part of your life — your work, your relationships, your peace.

Yes, struggles will return. But when they do, you'll recognize them for what they are:

Signs.

Stepping stones leading you toward the best version of yourself — the one who finally understands that love, faith, and growth are not destinations. They are the path itself.

Chapter 12

Religion

I was born into a deeply religious family. We went to church every Sunday — and often on weekdays too. Rain or shine, we lived, breathed, and slept religion. It shaped our meals, our mornings, our weekends, and our worldview.

Looking back, I now see religion in its simplest form as a practice of routine and discipline. Waking up early to exercise, eating meals on time, or brushing your teeth every morning — all of these are, in their own way, small religions. They are habits of devotion, rituals of consistency. I've often said that "brushing your teeth is a kind of religion." Few people agree, but I stand by it.

Most people, of course, think of religion as something formal — following a prophet or saint, attending church, mosque, or temple. But at its core, religion is about a shared set of beliefs about life, purpose, and community. It gives structure to chaos and offers comfort when logic runs out. In that sense, everyone has one — even if it's not tied to scripture or ceremony.

Religion and Spirituality: Overlaps and Distinctions

The words religion and spirituality often overlap. Both involve the search for meaning, truth, and connection to something greater than ourselves. But their approaches differ.

Religion is usually organized and communal. Spirituality is often personal and internal. Religion says, "Come join us." while Spirituality whispers, "Look within."

Years ago, while studying philosophy in university, I decided to explore this for myself. I visited churches of different denominations, several mosques, a few temples, and even a synagogue. Everywhere I went, I saw familiar patterns: singing, prayer, confession, giving, and seeking forgiveness. The languages differed, but the rhythm was the same — human beings reaching upward.

In the end, I realized that every religion I visited was teaching some version of self-control, community order, and moral structure. They weren't as different as their followers believed.

What My Cousin Taught Me

Before he passed, my cousin — a pastor and bishop — once told me, "Religion is the form spirituality takes in human civilizations."

At the time, I wasn't sure if he was right. Years later, I've come to believe he was — at least partly. Religion is the outer form, spirituality the inner essence. Religion is the vessel; spirituality is the water that fills it.

Philosophically, religion can be seen as a collection of cultural systems and symbols that connect humanity to moral and spiritual values. It gives meaning to life and builds a shared story about creation and destiny. Yet, every person must still walk their own path and reason through these truths independently. Blind belief is not enough — understanding must follow.

The Nature of Belief

Belief is not knowledge. To "believe" is to accept something as true without proof — and therefore to hold a shadow of doubt.

Faith and hope are beautiful, but they are not strategies. You cannot build your future on faith alone; it must rest on action, wisdom, and knowledge.

Knowledge brings love, and love brings truth. When you know something — really know — doubt disappears, and peace follows. That's what lifts you to a higher spiritual plane, where religion becomes less about rules and more about realization.

The Shape of Religion

Religion, in practice, has always been public. It involves organization, community, and ritual. Most major religions have formal hierarchies — pastors, priests, imams — along with scriptures, holy places, and ceremonies that mark the stages of life: birth, marriage, death, and renewal.

They may include:

- Sermons and readings from sacred texts
- Festivals and feasts celebrating divine acts or seasonal cycles
- Meditation and prayer to connect the mind and spirit
- Music, art, and dance as expressions of worship
- Rituals of passage — weddings, initiations, funerals

- Moral laws and customs that define belonging and behavior

The forms differ, but the purpose remains: to help human beings connect with the divine and with each other.

Religion Across Cultures

Some religions emphasize belief — adherence to doctrine. Others emphasize practice — daily living in alignment with certain values. Some focus on personal experience; others on community participation.

Certain traditions claim to be universal, binding on all of humanity; others are local, rooted in a tribe or culture. In many societies, religion became woven into public institutions: education, health care, government, even the family structure. Religion shaped art, law, and ethics — it still does.

At its best, religion gives meaning, purpose, and community. At its worst, it can be used for control. The difference lies in how it's practiced — whether as a tool for awakening, or a weapon for dominance.

My Truth

After all my searching — through churches, temples, and texts — I came to a simple conclusion:

Religion is humanity's language for talking to God.

Spirituality is God's language for talking back.

One is public, the other private. Both are needed.

But neither works without understanding — without love.

And love, I've learned, is the only true religion that never divides.

Chapter 13

God: the Divine Creator

For the sake of argument, let's agree on this: God and the universe are one and the same.

Call it energy, consciousness, or creation itself — every name points toward the same mystery.

"God" is the English word used for the singular being worshiped in most theistic religions — the one, supreme, creative force in the cosmos. Whether seen as the only deity in monotheism or as one divine aspect among many in polytheism, the idea of God has always shaped human understanding of existence.

Early Encounters with God

When I was a boy growing up back home, church was a weekly ritual — Sunday mornings, evening service, midweek meetings. Like most children, I didn't really understand why I was there. I had no concept of who or what God was. I went because my parents went.

At Sunday school, we dropped coins into the collection plate, and I remember asking my mother, "Why does God need money?" She smiled but never answered. The Bible, to me, was just another book — like the ones we studied in school — filled with stories that adults told us were sacred.

When I grew older and came to this country, not much changed. Every picture in the church, every image in the Bible, showed faces

that looked nothing like mine. Jesus, the saints, even the angels —
none resembled the people I knew. During Christmas dinners, we
prayed to thank Jesus for the food, but never the cook, the farmer,
or the animal that gave its life for our meal.

I had no personal relationship with God — only borrowed beliefs.
My understanding came from repetition, not revelation.

Awakening to a Larger Creator

It wasn't until university that I began to question what I'd been
taught. I started searching beyond the sermons — exploring
philosophy, culture, and the spiritual traditions of my ancestors. I
realized that God is not confined to a building, a book, or a picture
on a wall.

God is the divine spark within all creation — the living energy that
animates everything. I came to understand that the Creator
conceived and formed the universe itself — from the stars to the
smallest seed — and that every one of us carries that creative
essence. We are each, in our own way, a reflection of God's image.

If modern science tells us that the universe is millions of years old,
then the Creator must have existed long before time began — before
Rome, before Greece, before the first human words for "God."
Indigenous peoples across Africa, the Americas, and Asia were
invoking this divine force long before history was written, and they
didn't need intermediaries to do it.

The Word "God" — A Brief History

Many believe the earliest use of the word "God" comes from the Bible, but linguistics tells a broader story.

The English term God originates from the Proto-Germanic guđan, itself drawn from the Proto-Indo-European root ǵhau(ə)-, meaning "to call" or "to invoke."

In early Germanic traditions, the word was neutral — neither male nor female. It only became masculine during the Christianization of Europe. Across cultures, the name has many counterparts:

- Deus (Latin)
- Bog (Slavic)
- Ishvara / Deva (Sanskrit)
- Allah (Arabic)
- El / Yahweh (YHWH) (Hebrew)
- Achamán (among the Guanches of the Canary Islands)

Each name points to the same idea — a supreme creative presence that is called upon, invoked, and revered.

Conceptions of God

Across traditions, God is understood as the all-powerful, all-knowing, and ever-present creator. Philosophers and theologians have long described God as:

- Omniscient — all-knowing

- Omnipotent — all-powerful
- Omnipresent — everywhere
- Omnibenevolent — perfectly good
- Eternal and necessary — existing beyond time or cause

In other words, God is all things — within and beyond.

Some see God as incorporeal and immaterial; others as a personal being or the moral center of the universe. For many ancient and modern thinkers — Jewish, Christian, Muslim, African, or Eastern — God represents the greatest conceivable existence: the source from which all life flows.

The African Conception of God

Africa — the cradle of civilization — is also the root of much of humanity's earliest spiritual thought. Across the continent, countless cultures developed stories of creation that reveal deep reverence for divine power expressed through nature and ancestry.

Here are a few examples:

- Mbombo — among the Kuba people, the creator god who existed in darkness and, in pain, expelled the sun, moon, and stars from his being, forming the universe.
- Obatala — in Yoruba tradition, the creator of human beings, mountains, and valleys.
- Olorun — ruler of the sky and creator of the sun.

- Unkulunkulu — in Zulu myth, he rose from the reeds bringing with him people and cattle, shaping earth and life.
- Kibuka — the Baganda god of war, who descended as a cloud raining spears on his enemies.
- Menhit — the Egyptian goddess of war, believed to march before armies with fiery arrows.
- Tano — Ashanti goddess of strife and courage.
- Takhar — the Senegalese god of justice and vengeance, protector of the faithful.
- Shango — Yoruba god of thunder, whose voice was said to sound like lightning.
- Oya — his wife, goddess of wind and fire, guardian of the gates of death.
- Mukasa — god of wealth and abundance, worshipped near Lake Victoria.
- Aje and Oshun — deities of prosperity, love, and fertility in Yoruba belief.
- Njoku Ji — Igbo goddess of the yam and agricultural fertility.
- Mami Wata — goddess of wealth and water, bringing beauty, power, and fortune.
- Anubis — Egyptian god of death and protector of the afterlife.
- Ma'at — goddess of truth and balance, weighing the hearts

of the dead.

These are only a fraction of the vast pantheon of African deities — reflections of humanity's early attempts to understand and honor the creative forces of the world. Each story, each name, is a different window into the same mystery: the divine creative power that sustains life.

God in Other Cultures

Elsewhere, the Creator takes on new names and forms:

- In Hinduism, God is both personal and cosmic — known as Vishnu, Krishna, Ishvara, or Hari.
- In Judaism, God is referred to as El, Adonai, or YHWH — "the one who is."
- In Islam, Allah represents the all-compassionate and all-merciful creator.
- In Christianity, God manifests as Father, Son, and Holy Spirit — a trinity of unity and diversity.
- In Indigenous American beliefs, God takes countless forms: Achamán, Wakan Tanka, Great Spirit.

Though languages differ, the essence is constant — a supreme intelligence guiding all creation.

The Bible and the Names of God

Throughout the Hebrew and Christian scriptures, many names

describe the character of God:

- Elohim — "the mighty ones," a plural form suggesting majesty
- El Shaddai — "God Almighty"
- El Elyon — "God Most High"

Each name reveals a facet of the divine personality — strength, compassion, wisdom, justice.

Personally, I refer to God as the Creator or the Universe, depending on whom I'm speaking with. The language changes; the reverence does not.

My Understanding

Over the years, I've come to believe that God is not distant or confined to doctrine.

God is consciousness itself — present in all, through all, as all.

Every atom, every heartbeat, every act of creation bears the fingerprint of divinity.

To me, God is the spark that animates life, the law that governs balance, and the love that holds the universe together.

Theologians debate God's attributes. Philosophers ask, "Does God exist?"

But I no longer need to argue. I feel God in the quiet morning air, in laughter, in pain, in the simple fact that we are here — thinking, breathing, and creating.

The divine is not separate from us.

We are not searching for God — we are remembering.

Chapter 14

Religious View

In this chapter, I want to make a clear distinction between religion and God — two words that many people use interchangeably but that I see as entirely different, even unrelated.

Religion is human-made: a system of beliefs, rituals, and codes created to give structure to faith.

God, on the other hand, is existence itself — the source beyond systems, the divine presence within and around everything.

Theological Views of God

The great theologians of history have wrestled with defining the divine. Within the Abrahamic traditions, three dominant views have emerged:

- Judaism, which holds a strict monotheistic definition of God.
- Christianity, which presents a Trinitarian view — Father, Son, and Holy Spirit.
- Islam, which affirms a single, indivisible God — Allah.

The Dharmic religions of the East (Hinduism, Buddhism, Jainism, Sikhism) offer very different frameworks. In Hinduism, for example, the conception of God varies by region and tradition — from monotheistic to polytheistic to entirely non-theistic. The divine is not a single ruler, but a vast, interconnected reality that manifests in countless forms.

In most of these systems, even the gods themselves are seen as facilitators, not the final destination. They may help guide humans toward deliverance, but cannot replace individual effort on the path to enlightenment.

In modern times, more abstract theological concepts such as process theology, open theism, and panentheism have tried to explain God as a living, evolving force — one that moves within time and creation, rather than beyond it.

But despite all these perspectives, there is no universal consensus on what God actually is. Every believer, thinker, and culture adds another color to the canvas.

Philosophical Views of God

Philosophers have debated the existence of God for centuries — some attempting to prove it, others to disprove it. Their debates belong to two great fields of thought:

Epistemology (how we know things) and ontology (what truly exists).

Arguments for God's existence include:

- Metaphysical arguments — claiming that the very existence of the universe implies a creator.
- Empirical or inductive arguments — citing order and complexity in nature.
- Moral arguments — suggesting that moral law requires a

moral lawgiver.

Arguments against God's existence often rest on:

- The problem of evil (how a good God allows suffering).
- The lack of empirical evidence.
- The self-contradiction in defining a being that is omnipotent, omniscient, and benevolent all at once.

The Spectrum of Belief

From these philosophical struggles arise many positions along a spectrum:

- Strong atheism: "God does not exist."
- De facto atheism: "God almost certainly does not exist."
- Agnosticism: "No one knows whether God exists."
- Weak theism: "God exists, but cannot be proven."
- Strong theism: "God exists, and this can be proven."

There are countless variations between these points. Some thinkers hold that science and religion occupy non-overlapping domains — that science explores the natural world, while religion addresses meaning and morality. Others argue the two will always intersect, since both seek truth.

Free Will and Divine Intention

I personally believe that the human body is merely a vessel for the divine spirit — that life begins when the spirit takes its first breath and ends when it exhales its last.

In this view, the spirit uses the body to experience freedom on Earth. Human life becomes a temporary collaboration between the eternal and the physical.

Yet philosophers have long questioned whether free will can exist if God is all-knowing. If God already knows every future action, how can our choices be truly free?

If everything is predetermined, free will is an illusion. But if human freedom exists, then God may not know every future outcome — challenging the notion of omniscience.

Some reconcile this by saying that God knows all possibilities, but not which choice we will make until we make it. This preserves both divine knowledge and human freedom — though the debate is far from settled.

As philosopher Blaise Pascal famously said:

"The heart has its reasons which reason knows not of."

Faith, then, becomes not a conclusion of reason, but a leap of trust — an act of courage in the face of uncertainty.

Theism and Deism

Theism asserts that God exists as a real, independent being who created and sustains everything. God is both transcendent (beyond the world) and immanent (within the world). Theists usually believe

God is omnipotent, omniscient, and benevolent — yet these beliefs raise timeless questions about evil and suffering.

Open Theism offers a variation: because time unfolds moment by moment, even God experiences it dynamically. God knows all that can be known, but the future remains open.

Deism, by contrast, presents a detached Creator — one who designed the universe but no longer interferes with it. In Deism, there are no miracles, no answered prayers — only the laws of nature, set in motion long ago.

Monotheism and Religious Pluralism

Monotheists believe in one God — though they may use different names and traditions. Many even hold that all religions worship the same ultimate being in different ways.

Yet exclusivists claim theirs is the only true path, while pluralists accept that others may hold partial truths.

Relativistic inclusivism goes further, suggesting that salvation or enlightenment is eventually available to all, regardless of faith.

Syncretism blends traditions — as seen in New Age spirituality or Afro-Caribbean faiths that merge Christian and traditional African elements.

Pantheism and Its Variants

Pantheism holds that God is the universe — everything that exists is divine.

Panentheism says that God contains the universe but also exists beyond it — the ocean and the wave together.

Dystheism suggests that God may not be wholly good — a response to the problem of evil.

Non-theism removes the supernatural altogether, explaining the universe purely through natural laws.

Some non-theists view "God" as a metaphor for human ideals — a symbol of our longing for justice, beauty, and connection.

Science and Non-Religious Perspectives

Modern thinkers such as Stephen Jay Gould proposed the idea of Non-Overlapping Magisteria (NOMA) — that science and religion each govern separate realms:

Science explains how the world works; religion explores why it matters.

Science answers empirical questions. Religion and philosophy address meaning and morality.

In this framework, the absence of supernatural evidence does not disprove God — it simply defines science's boundaries.

Anthropomorphism and the Human Mirror

Across cultures, humans tend to imagine gods in their own image.

Ancient Greek deities quarreled, loved, and betrayed — just like us.

Anthropologists argue that we project human traits onto the divine because it makes the unknown familiar.

Freud went further, claiming that God is a projection of the father figure — a symbol of authority, protection, and punishment.

Sociologists add another layer: as human societies grew larger, gods became moral enforcers. In small groups, reputation and gossip maintained social order; in vast societies, the idea of ever-watchful gods helped enforce cooperation and morality.

In that sense, belief in divine oversight may have been humanity's earliest form of governance — the invisible eye that kept chaos at bay.

Final Reflection

Whether one views God as a being, a force, a metaphor, or a myth, the question itself continues to shape civilization.

Religion gave us order. Philosophy gave us inquiry. Science gave us explanation.

And perhaps, when all three finally meet — when belief, knowledge, and wonder find balance — we will not just argue about God's existence.

We will recognize that our search for God has always been our search for ourselves.

Chapter 15

My Views

After reading and thinking through all these religious, spiritual, and philosophical ideas, my eyes and brain feel like they're bleeding. There's simply too much to process. Still, if it all makes sense to you — great.

I've spent the last few chapters exploring Spirituality, Religion, and God to show how complex — and divisive — they can be. Everyone, everywhere, has an interpretation, and anyone can write or preach anything. If you're willing to accept the words of others without reflection, life may seem simple. But if you read deeply, question, and look between the lines, you'll see the hidden signs pointing toward truth.

Don't just accept the surface — search for meaning beneath it. Look long and deep. Seek the signals that resonate with your spirit.

And no, before you ask — I'm not saying that God could be a billy goat. But if you don't search for your own truth, you might end up following one.

So, check for yourself. Don't wait. Find the divine spark within you — the God in you. That's your true power.

Trust your intuition — your sixth sense. The signs are already in front of your mind's eye, waiting to be seen.

Chapter 16

The Hero

Hero /ˈhi(ə)rō/ — noun

A person admired for courage, outstanding achievements, or noble qualities.

We often think of heroes as characters in books, movies, or myths — people with extraordinary powers or divine lineage. But the truth is very much simpler and closer to home:

I am the only true hero I've ever met.

I can vividly remember when I tore my Achilles tendon and couldn't walk up the stairs, or the time when I ran out of gas in the middle of nowhere, and even when depression hugged me tightly and anger closed in on all my senses, it was me — I was the one there. Not a savior, not a sidekick — just me.

I was there when I fell and when I failed, when I broke down. and when I rose again.

There were moments I wanted to ask, "Why me, God? Why all this pain?" But then I remembered Job — the man in the Bible who lost everything yet never cursed God.

Job's story is one of endurance. God and Satan made a wager to test his faith. Satan stripped Job of everything — family, wealth, health — but Job remained steadfast. When the test was over, God restored him many times over.

And that's when it hit me: life itself is a test.

Life as a Test

Why me? Why you? Why any of us? It is because the universe is testing our character, our strength, and connection to the Creator.

How else could we know that our brains still think, our bodies still heal, and our spirits still rise?

Every hardship — the broken foot, the business collapse, the failed relationship, the eviction — it was a challenge hurled by the universe at me, its a question disguised as pain.

A chance to answer with resilience.

So I stopped asking why.

The "why" belongs to God.

The real question is how.

Ask "How," Not "Why"

When life gets rough, don't ask "Why is this happening to me?"

Ask "How do I get through this?"

How do I stretch the last dollar to Friday?

How do I overcome this heartbreak?

How do I stop this habit, this fear, this doubt?

That's where growth lives — in the how.

Through betrayal, rejection, disrespect, and loss, I discovered my own strength. When there was no one left to lean on, I became my own rescuer — my own doctor, mechanic, cook, and comforter.

I learned to fix what was broken — including myself.

The Hero in Everyday Life

In myths and history, heroes are soldiers, saints, or legends favored by gods. However, In modern times, heroes include first responders, healers, and innovators. But for most of us — those without capes, titles, or armies — heroism looks different.

The modern hero is the single mother who keeps going after a long shift.

The father who sacrifices his sleep to build a dream.

The student who studies by candlelight.

The person who refuses to quit, even when the world says "no."

We are all potential heroes — not because we save the world, but because we save ourselves.

Save Yourself

No army general, no superhero, no masked avenger is coming to rescue you. Not Spider-Man, not Superman, not the Bat guy.

You must save yourself.

Start with the person in the mirror — that's your hero.

Ask yourself the only question that matters:

How badly do I want it?

Do I want a better life?

Am I willing to do what it takes to build it?

If your answer is "no," then nothing changes.

But if your answer is "yes," then it's time to act.

I had to be my own hero. To push, fall, rise, and rebuild — again and again.

Every time my world collapsed — my business, my marriage, my finances — I learned patience, humility, and spiritual awareness. Each fall taught me something my comfort never could.

Lessons from Failure

I made mistakes — big ones. I rushed into relationships without thought, trusted too easily, invested unwisely. I tried to build castles on sand, and they all crumbled.

But each fall revealed the signs I had ignored. Each pain pointed me back to purpose.

To change my world, I first had to learn to live in the dark — to make the last dollar stretch, to rebuild from ashes, to find meaning in hardship. I had to quiet the noise, control my impulses, and learn patience.

I had to change my mind before I could change my life.

The Power of Intention

An old friend once told me, "Be mindful of your intentions." I didn't understand then, but I do now.

You can't start something with one motive and expect a different outcome halfway through. You can't marry for money and expect love. You can't build for greed and expect peace.

The intention you begin with shapes the destiny you end with.

My grandmother used to send me to the shop for a jug of milk. Sometimes, I came back with a cow. She'd look at me and laugh — "Boy, I asked for milk, not a cow!"she did;nt want to care for a cow.

That's how life works. Stay clear on your purpose from the start. Don't change the rules halfway through.

The Takeaway

Life is not about waiting for rescue.

It's about realizing that the hero has always been you.

Every setback is a training ground. Every pain is a signpost. Every test is a chance to rise stronger.

Stop asking "why me."

Start asking "how do I move forward."

Then do it.

Because in the end — you are your own hero

Chapter 17

Success

In my younger days, sitting in a noisy grade-school classroom, I had plenty of wishes. I wanted to be a professional basketball player. I just needed to be a little taller. I wished hard for height — it never came. I wished for that fine girl who seemed too good to be true — but she was already with someone else.

I learned early that wishing doesn't make things happen. Effort does.

So, what is success really?

If I were to ask ten people, I'd likely get ten different answers. Over time, I've come to understand success not as a destination but as the ability to rise after each fall, to face the universe's endless tests and still find the will to move forward. Success is landing on your feet — sometimes gracefully, often barely — after tumbling through chaos.

It's overcoming predictable and unpredictable losses.

It's narrowly escaping failure and learning from every scrape.

There's a saying that someone who "lands on their feet" does so out of luck. Maybe. But if luck finds you, it's because you stayed in the game long enough for it to show up. You earned it.

The Addiction of Achievement

Success, I've found, is a kind of drug. The chase becomes an addiction — the high of the climb, the thrill of the risk, the rush of conquering fear.

To pursue success is to crave challenge. It's to face the mountain, tumble down it, bleed, and then start climbing again.

No, I've never smoked or injected anything for a high — but I know the rush of chasing success. Each taste of victory is fleeting, and every next one is harder to reach. That's what keeps us hungry.

To reach even half of your goals, you must master unshakable focus. You must sweat, bleed, and fight. You must become comfortable with failure, even friendly with it.

If you're afraid to fail, you're really afraid to succeed.

So go ahead — risk your money, your time, your comfort. Bend rules if you must, lose friends if you have to. Success requires sacrifice. Playing it safe is for chickens. Comfort is the enemy of greatness.

You have to grow up, stop following the crowd, and give up that childlike fear of falling.

Final Words

"Change your mind and you will change your life."

That's not just a saying — it's the truth. No one can change you but you.

Open your mind to the signs around you. Listen to the quiet voice of the universe. Whether you're battling depression, addiction, heartbreak, rejection, financial ruin, or self-doubt — the first step out of darkness begins in your own mind.

I've been there.

Worn out. Broke. Sitting on the couch, stunned, watching my world disappear. The house emptied. The dreams shattered. I didn't know whether to scream, cry, or help them move the furniture out.

I just sat there — silent — and then I moved on.

Years later, I realized that moment wasn't the end. It was the turning point. It changed everything.

The Hard Truth About Failure

I've lost more money than I care to admit. I've failed more times than I can count.

But I remember reading about the man credited with inventing the light bulb — how he failed a thousand times. When asked why he didn't quit, he said, "I now know a thousand ways not to fail."

That struck me deeply.

I've fallen off my own mountain again and again, bruised and broken, but never beaten. I've rebuilt my life from zero more times than I can remember. The pain was crushing — physical, emotional, spiritual — but I never waved the white flag.

Quitting has never been an option.

I've lived through the exhaustion, the dark days, the sleepless nights.

I've seen the bank account hit zero — even negative. I've pumped twenty dollars of gas and watched the needle barely move. I've eaten in silence, walked in the cold, and slept in cars and storage units.

I've known the sting of abandonment and the weight of shame. I've been treated as less — judged as a failure by people who couldn't see past the moment.

But here's what they didn't see:

Each loss was a lesson. Each failure was a signpost.

The bruises, the scars, the overdrafts — they were all messages from the universe saying, "Keep going"

The Real Signs of Success

So don't lose heart. The universe is always sending signs — subtle, persistent, and sometimes painful — pointing toward your growth.

If I can survive and rebuild, you can too.

You just have to look for the signs. They're everywhere — on the walls, in the faces of strangers, in the mirror, in your breath.

When you see one that reads "Have Courage — 50 Feet Ahead,"

run toward it.

You'll need it.

Gratitude

Along the way, I've met good people who believed in me when I did not know or couldn't believe in myself — the gas station clerk who let me fill up and pay later, the landlord who gave me another month, the friend who didn't turn away.

To them, I owe my deepest thanks.

I've never paused to grade myself on how well I'm doing on this test called life. But the fact that I'm still here — still getting up, still working, still writing these words — is proof enough that I'm passing.

I'm still learning to read the signs.

And maybe, that's what real success looks like.

Epilogue:
The Signs of Greatness

When I look back on every fall, every heartbreak, every failure and rise, I see the same message echoing through it all: the signs were always there.

They were in the silence between breaths, in the sleepless nights, in the strange coincidences that turned into turning points. I missed them sometimes — often — but they never stopped showing up.

Each storm that shook my life wasn't punishment; it was preparation. Each closed door wasn't rejection; it was redirection. The universe was teaching me a language that can't be spoken, only felt — the language of signs.

Now I know: greatness is not a destination or a trophy. It's the quiet decision to rise again. It's gratitude after loss, peace after chaos, strength after surrender.

Greatness is born in the dark — when you finally trust that the light will find you again.

So when you stand at your next crossroad, listen. The universe still speaks. The signs are there. They always have been.

And this time, maybe you'll see them.

THE END

About The Author

A. Mustafa Tut Brown Jr

Mustafa Tut Brown Jr. is a Life & Business Coach, Mental Health and Addiction Counselor, an Independent Film Producer, a closet musician, and a Serial Entrepreneur based in Toronto, Ontario, Canada.

He is a father of six, he draws his deepest motivation from family, using his own journey to inspire others to see more, be more, and do more—for themselves, their loved ones, and their communities.

Since 1987, Tut-Brown has walked a diverse entrepreneurial path: Auto sales, lease and finance dealer, trucking owner and driver, of a few cargo transport companies, and demolition contractor. A kitchen and cabinetry sales professional, construction and renovation general contractor, financial consultant, and business and personal advisor, among others.

The road has been demanding, rocky to say the least, but he embraces every challenge in each chapter of it. In his words, he "would not change a thing" and fully owns his story—successes, failures, and everything in between.

In 2006, after going through personal and business bankruptcy and spending a period living in his car, Tut-Brown experienced a turning point. He realized that his true calling had always been there: helping people navigate their challenges, find solutions, and move toward their best selves. What he had done naturally for years—as a counselor, problem-solver, and coach—became the foundation of his life's work.

As a life coach, his intention is simple but profound: to help people "awaken the hero within themselves." He challenges others to move beyond lazy thinking and inaction, to reject mediocrity, fear, doubt, and disbelief, and to step into a larger vision of who they can become. His work, including Addict, Signs, & Sayings, is dedicated to every person willing to confront their truth and rewrite their story.

www.ingramcontent.com/pod-product-compliance
Lightning Source LLC
Chambersburg PA
CBHW051301120626
46547CB00015B/2035